RUSKIN AND
VIOLLET-LE-DUC

THIS IS THE FIRST OF THE
WALTER NEURATH MEMORIAL LECTURES
WHICH WILL BE GIVEN ANNUALLY EACH SPRING ON
SUBJECTS REFLECTING THE INTERESTS OF
THE FOUNDER
OF THAMES AND HUDSON

THE DIRECTORS WISH TO EXPRESS
PARTICULAR GRATITUDE TO THE GOVERNORS AND
MASTER OF BIRKBECK COLLEGE,
UNIVERSITY OF LONDON,
FOR THEIR GRACIOUS SPONSORSHIP OF
THESE LECTURES

RUSKIN AND VIOLLET-LE-DUC

ENGLISHNESS AND FRENCHNESS IN THE APPRECIATION OF GOTHIC ARCHITECTURE

NIKOLAUS PEVSNER

THAMES AND HUDSON
LONDON

This lecture was given in memory of Walter Neurath, born in 1903, who founded Thames and Hudson, and who made it the leading publishing house in England for books on art. Some people, with intent to wound, call them coffee-table books. The term in my opinion does not justify any pejorative undertones. It simply means large books with plenty of illustrations. Now I can think back of the time when Basil Clarke's 'Church Builders of the Nineteenth Century' came out (in 1938) with a total of thirty-two plates, and Geoffrey Grigson's 'Samuel Palmer, the Visionary Years' (in 1947) with eighteen illustrations, and my illustrious colleague's at Birkbeck College, Sir John Summerson's book on Christopher Wren without any. Compare that with that wonderful book edited by Joan Evans and called 'The Flowering of the Middle Ages', its outstanding texts by the foremost experts and its 631 illustrations, or its companion pieces on 'The Dawn of Civilization', with Stuart Piggott as its editor and on 'The Dark Ages' with David Talbot Rice as its editor. True, such books are a little heavy for bed or tube, but would you rather have less pictures or smaller ones? Besides, there are Thames and Hudson books of handy format and just as excellent in their scholarly texts, the volumes of 'Ancient Peoples and Places' for instance, over fifty now, edited by Glyn Daniel.

No — Walter Neurath was our benefactor, though of course he managed by the skilful manipulating of international co-operation not to be without profits either; but he who chose these topics and these authors and editors was a man of vision and courage. As far as I am concerned, he was very good to me and made the collection of my essays something much more impressive than

5

their texts alone could ever have been. So when I think back to Walter Neurath, I do so with a feeling of gratitude to him and his staff.

And if now this memorial lecture has been established by Eva Neurath, Thomas Neurath and the other directors and will in future be held once a year, I hope you will notice even in the choice of my subject the recognition that Walter Neurath did not confine himself to the obvious and saw very sharply the possibilities of the far from obvious. You will have to decide whether my subject has possibilities, but I venture to think that Walter Neurath, were he still with us, would in the end approve.

1 *John Ruskin in 1853, aged thirty-four: portrait by John Everett Millais*

2 Eugène Viollet-le-Duc in 1840, aged twenty-six

Master, Ladies and Gentlemen,

I have two actors, and I must introduce them to you, though you might say that Ruskin needs no introduction. Viollet-le-Duc, however, does. He was born in 1814, Ruskin in 1819. Viollet-le-Duc died in 1879, Ruskin only in 1900, but Ruskin was out of his mind from 1889 to his death, and had outbreaks of his mental illness first in 1878 and then several more in the next ten years. Ruskin's operative books on architecture are *The Seven Lamps of Architecture*, published in 1849, *The Stones of Venice*, published in two volumes in 1851 and 1853, and the Edinburgh *Lectures on Architecture and Painting* published in 1854.[1] Viollet-le-Duc's operative works are the *Dictionnaire raisonné de l'architecture française* of 1854–68 and the *Entretiens sur l'architecture* of 1863 and 1872. So nearly all I have to tell you belongs to the twenty or twenty-five High Victorian years.

Both men were Gothic enthusiasts, and both worshipped the same phase, the High Gothic, or as the Victorians said, the Middle Pointed, of the thirteenth century – in France the age of Reims and Amiens, in England (with a certain time-lag) that of Westminster Abbey and the fifty years after the rebuilding of the Abbey had begun.

Both men were also enthusiasts of stone and hence of geology. The fourth volume of *Modern Painters* is largely concerned with geology,[2] and Viollet-le-Duc actually wrote a book on Mont Blanc.[3] He was as fervent a devotee of the Alps as was Ruskin, and as an active climber he found himself on an expedition in 1870 trapped in a crevasse and was only rescued by good luck.[4]

Ruskin's reaction to the Alps cannot be demonstrated better than by quoting a passage from *The Seven Lamps*:

Among the hours of his life to which the writer looks back with peculiar gratitude, as having been marked by more than ordinary fulness of joy or clearness of teaching, is one passed, now some years ago, near time of sunset, among the broken masses of pine forest which skirt the course of the Ain, above the village of Champagnole, in the Jura. It is a spot which has all the solemnity, with none of the savageness, of the Alps; where there is a sense of a great power beginning to be manifested in the earth, and of a deep and majestic concord in the rise of the long low lines of piny hills; the first utterance of those mighty mountain symphonies, soon to be more loudly lifted and wildly broken along the battlements of the Alps. But their strength is as yet restrained; and the far-reaching ridges of pastoral mountain succeed each other, like the long and sighing swell which moves over quiet water from some far-off stormy sea. And there is a deep tenderness pervading that vast monotony. The destructive forces and the stern expression of the central ranges are alike withdrawn. No frost-ploughed, dust-encumbered paths of ancient glacier fret the soft Jura pastures; no splintered heaps of ruin break the fair ranks of her forest; no pale, defiled, or furious rivers send their rude and changeful ways among her rocks. Patiently, eddy by eddy, the clear green streams wind along their well-known beds; and under the dark quietness of the undisturbed pines, there spring up, year by year, such company of joyful flowers as I know not the like of among all the blessing of the earth.[5]

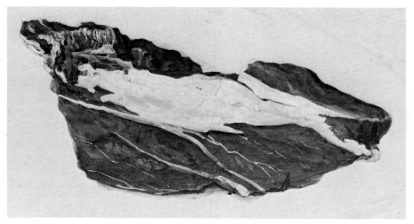

3 Ruskin's geological studies: piece of rock with quartz veining

4, 5 *Ruskin's studies of Alpine scenery: (above) mountain rocks and Alpine rose, and (below) pine forest on Mont-Cenis*

6 Ruskin:
Glacier des Bossons,
Chamonix

12

Now here we have the first contrast between Ruskin and Viollet-le-Duc. Ruskin was a writer, Viollet-le-Duc a doer. In 1830 Viollet was on the barricades; Ruskin's social criticism never got near instigation to violent action, as William Morris's did. Ruskin, when it came to action such as in founding the St George's Guild in 1871 or building the Hinksey Road or re-establishing wool spinning at Laxey in 1876 and the linen industry in Langdale in 1884, was ineffectual; Viollet-le-Duc was a competent but not an inspired writer. The same exactly is true of the two as draughtsmen. Ruskin's drawings are always satisfying and often brilliant, Viollet conveys very well what he has to convey but rarely reaches above that level, although he drew much for Baron Taylor and Nodier's *Voyages pittoresques* in 1838 and the following years.

Ruskin called Viollet-le-Duc 'for art 800–1200 the best-informed, most intelligent and most thoughtful of guides' and the *Dictionnaire* 'noble'.[6] Viollet-le-Duc never seems to have mentioned Ruskin, but

7 *Building the Hinksey Road*

Cathédrale d'Amiens.
Chœur

13 Ruskin: part of the façade of the Doge's Palace, Venice

20

14 *Viollet-le-Duc:*
diagram of a Venetian palazzo
(detail)

Let us examine Ruskin's arguments first. They pervade *The Seven Lamps* and are expressed most beautifully in the chapter called 'The Nature of Gothic' in *The Stones of Venice*. To Ruskin the quality of architecture represents the quality of man. This applies to the designer as much as to the craftsman responsible for decorating buildings. 'A foolish person builds foolishly, and a wise one, sensibly; a virtuous one, beautifully; and a vicious one, basely.'[22] This is the one aspect, the other is: 'The right question to ask respecting all ornament is simply this: was it done with enjoyment – was the carver happy, while he was about it ?'[23]

On the whole Ruskin says much less about the designer than about the craftsman; for it is his conviction that architecture as distinguished from mere building is not a matter of design but of ornament: Architecture, he writes in *The Seven Lamps*, is that which imposes on building 'certain characters venerable or beautiful, but otherwise unnecessary'. His example is the breastwork of a castle: 'No one would call the laws architectural which determine the height of a breastwork or the position of a bastion. But if to the stone facing of that bastion be added an unnecessary feature, as a cable moulding, *that* is architecture.'[24] Once this is accepted, it follows that sculpture and painting are 'the entire masters of architecture', and that 'what we call architecture is only the association of these in noble masses or the placing of them in fit places. All architecture other than this is mere building . . . no exertion of the powers of high art.'[25]

Now – to complicate matters – Ruskin had another *idée fixe* which is that carving and painting can be high art only if they are 'the carving or painting natural objects'[26] and sound judgement of the quality of carving and painting therefore 'founds itself on knowledge of nature'.[27]

Hence Ruskin's 'Nature of Gothic' is really the craftsman's breviary. 'The architect [should] work in the mason's yard with his men.'[28] The categories under which Ruskin sees the Gothic style are craftsman's categories. The first is 'Rudeness or savageness'[29] show‹ ing itself in imperfection. 'No architecture can be truly noble which

15 *Ruskin: Iris Florentina*

is *not* imperfect.' 'Imperfection is in some sort essential to all that we know of life. It is the sign . . . of a state of progress and change.'[30] Changefulness in fact qualifies as a separate category. It is demonstrated by 'the perpetual variety of every feature of a building'.[31] Hence, of course, naturalism or 'the love of natural objects for their own sake and the effort to represent them frankly, unconstrained by artistic laws'.[32] Next 'the sense of the Grotesque', i.e. 'the tendency to delight in fantastic and ludicrous, as well as in sublime, images'.[33] Of this Ruskin says little in 'The Nature of Gothic'. Fifth an 'active rigidity; the peculiar energy which gives tension to movement'. It is in fact 'a stiffness analogous to that of the bones of a limb, or fibres of a tree, a . . . communication of force from part to part'.[34] Finally redundance, i.e. 'the uncalculating bestowal of the wealth of . . . labour'. This richness, Ruskin adds, is 'a part of its humility'. For no architecture is so haughty as that which is simple'.[35]

You see how marvellously Ruskin can express subtle qualities and how justly he felt about the Gothic style. But it is all feeling, not reasoning. And so is the final summing-up, although this is where Ruskin sets out to teach how Gothic architecture can be recognized – but not its phases by recognition of detail, as a scholar would try to do, but again its quality:

24

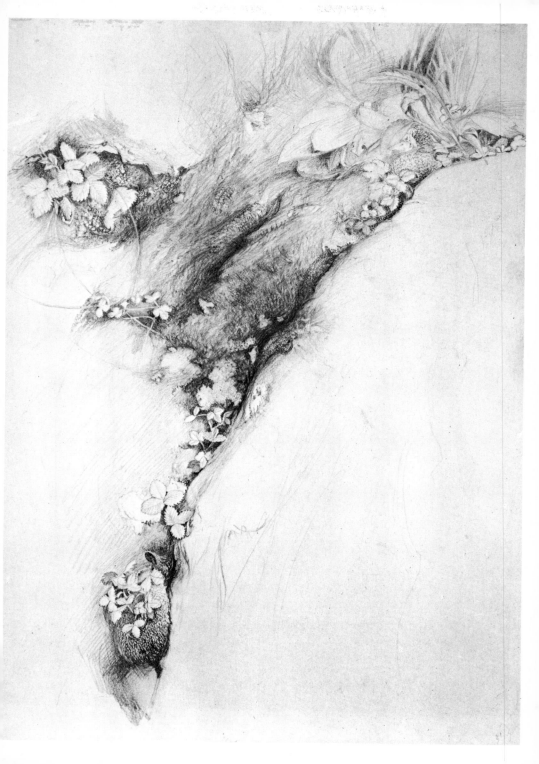

First, See if it looks as if it had been built by strong men; if it has the sort of roughness, and largeness, and nonchalance, mixed in places with the exquisite tenderness which seems always to be the sign-manual of the broad vision, and massy power of men who can see *past* the work they are doing, and betray here and there something like disdain for it. If the building has this character, it is much already in its favour; it will go hard but it proves a noble one.

Secondly, Observe if it be irregular, its different parts fitting themselves to different purposes, no one caring what becomes of them, so that they do their work. If one part always answers accurately to another part, it is sure to be a bad building; and the greater and more conspicuous the irregularities, the greater the chances are that it is a good one.

Thirdly, Observe if all the traceries, capitals and other ornaments are of perpetually varied design. If not, the work is assuredly bad.

Lastly, *Read* the sculpture.[36]

So the end of the chapter is again sculpture not architecture. But the beginning is Life: 'Pointed arches do not constitute Gothic, nor vaulted roofs, nor flying buttresses, nor grotesque sculptures; but all or some of these things, and many other things with them, when they come together so as to have life.'[37] He had said the same already in *The Seven Lamps*: 'Things are noble or ignoble in proportion to [their] fulness of life.'[38] That is the message of the Lamp of Life. With the Lamps of Sacrifice and of Truth I have already dealt. The Lamp of Beauty – of this I have also spoken – is concerned with ornament and with the relation of natural forms and abstraction in it. But a few words must still be said of the Lamps of Memory and Obedience; for it is here that Ruskin roams most wildly through his universe and moves furthest from the world of Viollet. 'It is in becoming memorial or monumental that a true perfection is attained by civil and domestic buildings.'[39] 'The greatest glory of a building is not in its stones, nor in its gold. It is in its age.'[40] This is why Ruskin, as you will hear later, felt so intensely about the preservation of old buildings.

But what has he to tell us of new buildings? What should their style be? 'A day never passes without our having our English archi-tects called upon to be original and to invent a new style. . . . We

want no new style of architecture. . . . It does not matter one marble splinter whether we have an old or new architecture. . . . The forms of architecture already known are good enough for us, and far better than any of us. . . . A man who has the gift, will take up any style that is going . . . and will work in that, and be great in that.'[41] But what style should be going? Ruskin's answer is surprising: 'The choice would lie, I think, between four styles', and they are '1. the Pisan Romanesque; 2. the early Gothic of the Western Italian

19 'The early Gothic of the Western Italian republics': Santa Maria della Spina, Pisa

Republics; 3. the Venetian Gothic in its general development; 4. the English earliest decorated',[42] and in the end evidently Ruskin does not even want to leave that choice, which incidentally means under 2, Florence and Siena and specially Giotto's Campanile, and under 3, the Doge's Palace; for he also writes this: 'Architecture never could flourish except when it was subjected to a national law as strict and as minutely authoritative as the laws which regulate religion, policy, and social relations.' What must be done therefore is 'to choose a style, and to use it universally'.[43] For Ruskin it would have been number 3, but England in the persons of Pugin, Scott and others had already decided for 4. In any case neither they nor Ruskin even considered a new style, an original style for their century.

28

20 'The Venetian Gothic in its general development': Casa Contarini-Fasan, Venice

Viollet-le-Duc on the other hand did, though in just as warped a way. His ideal – I have already said this – was also what Ruskin called the earliest decorated and others the Second or Middle Pointed, the style of Reims, Amiens, Westminster Abbey and a little later. But to Viollet, being politically a radical and religiously an agnostic, this style had to be the work of an 'école laïque'[44] developed by laymen (like Ruskin's carvers) and in opposition to monkery and all imposed authority. 'Les arts appartenaient au peuple et personne ne songeait à les diriger.'[45] That came in only with Louis XIV and the academies.

But whereas the independent creator of the great cathedrals to Ruskin was a rough craftsman, to Viollet he was a highly intelligent designer. For Gothic architecture is 'based absolutely on reason and science',[46] and in his *Dictionnaire*, throughout all the volumes, he did more than anyone had done before him to prove how rationally and ingeniously Gothic churches were constructed. In this, as Dr Middleton has demonstrated,[47] he was only following in the footsteps of earlier French theorists, of Delorme in the sixteenth, Derand in the seventeenth, Cordemoy and Frézier in the eighteenth century.

This very rationalism was one of Viollet-le-Duc's arguments in recommending Gothic for new buildings. The other – always in defence against the Classicism and Italianism of the Academy – was that Gothic was the national style of France.[48] Not that he recommended imitation, though in his own churches he practised it. What he wrote at the beginning of the *Entretiens* was: 'le passé est passé mais il faut le fouiller avec soin . . . s'attacher non pas à le faire revivre, mais à le connaître, pour s'en servir'.[49]

In fact, one has to distinguish between Viollet thinking of churches and thinking of secular buildings. Most of his radical and indeed seminal pronouncements must have referred in his mind to buildings other than religious. Here is an example: What we need is 'une alliance de la forme avec les besoins et avec les moyens de construction'. We must be truthful to 'le programme [et] les procédés de construction'. We must 'remplir . . . scrupuleusement les conditions

21 Viollet-le-Duc: façade of Saint-Denys-de-l'Estrée, Saint-Denis

22 Viollet-le-Duc: interior of Saint-Denys-de-l'Estrée, Saint-Denis

imposés par un besoin'. We must 'employer les matériaux suivant leur qualités et leur propriétés',[50] or to put it at its briefest: 'Pour faire une boite il est bon connaître ce qu'elle doit contenir.'[51] It is nonsense to give all houses in a square identical façades (à la Place Vendôme); it is nonsense to give a façade all identical windows, if the rooms inside serve different functions; it is nonsense to make the façade of a town hall similar to that of a church or to give a church an exterior which contradicts the interior (à la Madeleine) and so on.[52] Instead we ought to be fully aware all the time that 'on possède aujourd'hui des ressources immenses fournies par l'industrie et la facilité des transports'.[53] The engineers who have given us the railway engines have never dreamt of copying horse-drawn carriages. If the architects today do not want to help in the annihilation of their own profession, they must become 'des constructeurs habiles, prêts à profiter de toutes les ressources que fournit notre état social'.[54]

Set against this sweeping optimism of Viollet-le-Duc, Ruskin's hatred of the age, and especially his hatred of its *état social*. From 1857 onwards his theory of art and architecture became for a while largely bitter social criticism. 'It is the vainest of affectations to try and put beauty into shadows, while all real things that cast them are left to deformity.'[55] Hence the St George's Guild, the Hinksey Road and so on. But they were all amateurish attempts, and the savage style of his writing did far more for his cause:

Every kind of sordid, foul or venomous work which, in other countries, men dreaded or disdained, it should be England's duty to do – becoming thus the offscourer of the earth and taking the hyena instead of the lion upon her shield.[56]

The worship of the Immaculate Virginity of Money, mother of the Omnipotence of Money, is the Protestant form of Madonna worship.[57]

Stupidity is always the basis of the Judas bargain. We do great injustice to Iscariot, in thinking him wicked above all common wickedness. He was only a common money-lover, and, like all money-lovers, did not understand Christ; – could not make out the worth of Him, or meaning of Him. He never thought He would be killed. He was horror-struck when he found that Christ would be killed; threw his money away instantly, and hanged himself. . . . Judas was a common, selfish, muddle-headed, pilfering fellow; . . . Helpless to understand Christ, he yet believed in Him, much more than most of us do; had seen Him do miracles, thought He was quite strong enough to shift for Himself, and he, Judas, might as well make his own little bye-perquisites out of the affair. Christ would come out of it well enough, and he have his thirty pieces.[58]

If this is how Ruskin saw the England of his time, no wonder that he was especially fierce on the new building materials, on iron and glass, and on the new building functions such as railway stations. On using railways he wrote: 'No one would travel in that manner who could help it', and on the stations: 'Better bury gold in the embankments than put it in ornament in the stations',[59] and even more cuttingly at the very start of chapter one of *The Seven Lamps* he used as examples of non-architecture: 'a wasp's nest, a rat-hole or a railway station'.[60] Then on iron: 'The moment that iron in the least

33

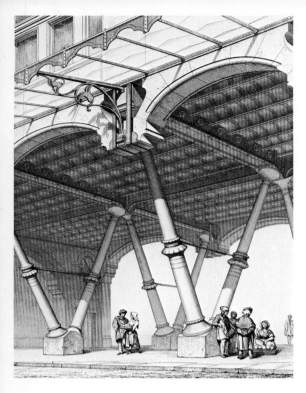

23, 24 Viollet-le-Duc's projects using dramatically exposed ironwork: (left) a market place and (right) a vaulted hall

degree takes the place of stone . . . the building ceases . . . to be true architecture.'[61] Ruskin's statement is in fact much more involved and includes the inconsistent prophecy that 'the time is probably near when a new system of architectural laws will be developed, adapted entirely to metallic construction'.[62] Yet 'The iron roofs and pillars of our railway stations . . . are not architecture at all.'[63]

Now compare with this Viollet-le-Duc and first of all some of the illustrations of the second volume of the *Entretiens*. There you have iron exposed demonstratively and dramatically, for supports of wide-spanning vaults and for ribs as well. Not that Viollet was the pioneer of this. Labrouste had exposed his iron piers and iron roof construction in the Bibliothèque Ste Geneviève in 1843–50, and Boileau had built several churches with iron piers and iron ribs in the fifties,

34

25, 26 Viollet-le-Duc's more conventional designs for actual buildings: (left) flats in the Rue de Douai, Paris and (right) project for the Opéra, Paris

best-known among them St Eugène in Paris of 1854–5.[64] The text which corresponds to Viollet's plates confirms them, and long calcu-lations of cost are introduced to convince readers. Also, architects are encouraged to look for forms which suit the qualities of iron and its manufacturing.[65] Nor should iron be used for wide spans only; in private houses floors, wall panels and staircases might be made of iron.[66] An additional advantage of iron, Viollet recognizes, is that the members can be made 'entièrement à l'atelier' and assembled on

36

the site.[67] This, of course, is the advantage Paxton discovered when he designed the Crystal Palace in 1850, the building Ruskin sneered at. According to him it was no more than 'a greenhouse larger than ever greenhouse was built before' and all that it needed in addition was 'some very ordinary algebra'.[68]

There you have the two men, but whereas Viollet here appears wholly forward-looking, Ruskin wholly backward-looking, examine some of Viollet's designs for buildings and you find him devoid of the courage of his words and drawings, whether you look at houses by him or his design of 1860 for the Opéra.

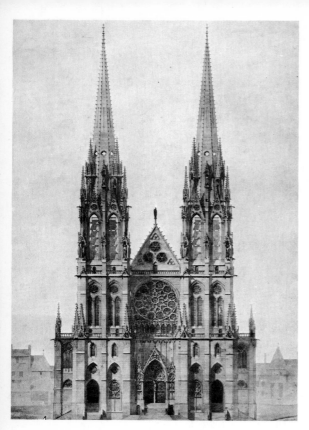

27 Viollet-le-Duc:
design for the façade of Clermont-Ferrand
Cathedral

28, 29 Pierrefonds,
before and after restoration

But there is one more, one final aspect of the two where the places are reversed. It is the restoration of old buildings. Viollet-le-Duc was the busiest restorer of France, of cathedrals as well as castles and ancient towns (Pierrefonds and the walls of Carcassonne are perhaps the best-known examples). Ruskin wrote of restoration: 'Restoration . . . means the most total destruction which a building can suffer.'[69] Nor was Viollet-le-Duc even as faithful a restorer as one might have expected. In the *Dictionnaire* he wrote: 'To restore a building is not just to preserve it, to repair it, and to remodel it, it is to re-instate it in a complete state such as it may never have been in at any given moment.'[70] And he acted accordingly. Great scholar that he was,

38

30-32 Carcassonne: (top) Viollet-le-Duc's sketch of the walls before restoration, (centre) his proposals for rebuilding and (below) the town as it now is

familiar with all the features and all the details of all the phases of medieval architecture, when in 1864–5 it came to lengthening the nave of Clermont-Ferrand Cathedral and to give it a west front, he disregarded the date of the nave – 1340–59 – and made the façade early- to mid-thirteenth-century in style.

Ruskin, of course, was driven to his radical statement by feeling much more deeply than Viollet-le-Duc ever did what it is that moves us in looking at a Gothic building. It is, you have seen, 'the life as a whole, the spirit which is given only by the hand and eye of the workman'.[71] Remove the surface and you have killed the building. That of course would not apply to a Greek temple or a Palladian mansion of the eighteenth century. But they did not concern either Ruskin or Viollet. So while Viollet went on restoring and remodelling till he died, Ruskin could see a few years before Viollet's death his principle of preservation instead of restoration coming to full fruition in the establishment of the Society for the Protection of Ancient Buildings. The date of the foundation of this society which is still going strong is 1877, and the founder was Ruskin's greatest pupil William Morris.

So here is a line from Ruskin to our century, just as strong as that from Viollet-le-Duc's iron supports. But Viollet's topical significance is for new, Ruskin's for old buildings. Moreover, Viollet's approach to the Gothic style is rational, Ruskin's emotional. That is where their Frenchness and Englishness lie. The direct succession from Delorme to Viollet has already been pointed out; there is just as direct one from Wren's arguments about building Gothic occasionally, by way of Thomas Gray and Horace Walpole, by way of the Gothic novel, and even by way of Pugin. However, since Pugin was of French descent, the emotional and the rational mix in him.

There is no such mixture in Ruskin. He is unreasonable throughout but not for that less forceful. So he won the battle for the protection of ancient buildings, as Viollet won that for the courageous use of the new materials.

Why then is it that he could not, in suggesting iron, himself use the new forms which the material called for ? Why could not Pugin, nor Scott nor Burges nor Robert Kerr, all of whom spoke up for iron and the need for a new style ? And why could no one else, except a horticulturist like Paxton, the engineers of the bridges, a naval engineer such as he who designed the boat-store at Sheerness and, true, some architects who remained obscure, such as Peter Ellis ?[72] Why this discrepancy of thought and performance ? In trying in conclusion to give an answer, I know that I am leaving safe ground. So what follows must be taken as no more than suggestions.

In nineteenth-century painting the split is familiar between progressive and traditional, novel and eclectic, unwelcome and welcome. In architecture there is no progressive and novel school, because there cannot be wholly unwelcome architecture. The painter can

42

lock himself up in his studio, paint and starve; if the architect has no client, there is no architecture. Hence architecture attracts men readier for a compromise with the world as they find it. The proposals of Viollet-le-Duc in words and drawings may be regarded as self-justification for Gothic restoring and eclectic building.

Or is this explanation too sophisticated? Is it all simpler, and can one suggest that, as the Georgian age had been conventional in its architectural style, so was the Victorian, and that radicalism became possible (for various reasons) only after 1890 or even 1900, but that radical thought always precedes radical action – not only in the French Revolution?

In choosing my subject for this first Walter Neurath lecture one reason I had was to ask these questions with some evidence; another was to demonstrate in the persons of Ruskin and Viollet-le-Duc traditional attitudes to architecture. But I have a third which I must now confess. Ruskin was Slade Professor at Oxford; so am I just at present. And Ruskin lectured to the Working Men's College, and my regular lecturing is to a Mechanics' Institute; for this is what Birkbeck College was when Dr Birkbeck founded it in 1823. It was at the Working Men's College that Ruskin met George Allen who then became his publisher, and this is what Ruskin wrote to Allen on the 15th of April 1878: 'How good and kind you are and have always been. I write this letter with solemn thanks for all the energy and faith of your life.'[73]

I need not say why I consider the quotation of this letter the most appropriate end to my Neurath Lecture.

NOTES

1 All my quotations are from E. T. Cook and A. Wedderburn: *The Complete Works of John Ruskin*, 39 vols, 1903–12, known as the Library Edition.

2 The volume was published in 1856. It is *Lib. Ed.* VI. Moreover, *Lib. Ed.* XXVI is entirely devoted to Ruskin's writings on geology, nearly all of the sixties, seventies and eighties.

3 *Le Massif du Mont Blanc*, Paris 1876. Ruskin read it and writes of it, *Lib. Ed.* XXVI, 221.

4 See *Eugène Viollet-le-Duc*, Catalogue of an exhibition held in 1965 and published by the Caisse Nationale des Monuments Historiques. The standard biography is Paul Gout, 1914. Dr Robin Middleton's excellent Ph.D. thesis, *Viollet-le-Duc and the Rational Gothic Tradition* (Cambridge 1957), has unfortunately never been converted into a book.

5 I am quoting this from Sir Kenneth Clark's wholly admirable *Ruskin Today*, London 1964, also existing as a Pelican book. It is an anthology and could not be bettered in selection as in commentary.

6 *Lib. Ed.* XXV, 502.

7 'L'article qu'il avait préparé sur Ruskin ne semble pas avoir été composé' – Pierre Trahard, *La Vieillesse de Prosper Mérimée*, 1930 (p. 58). Trahard refers to *Revue des Autographes*, January 1894, No. 163, and Chambon, *Lettres Inédites*, p. xiv. There was also a book published in 1860 called *L'esthétique anglaise, étude sur M John Ruskin*, by Joseph Milsand. The latest study of the subject is Jean Autrel, *Ruskin and the French before Proust*, Geneva, 1965. Renato De Fusco devotes the first chapter of his *L'Idea dell'Architettura,* Milan, 1964, to Viollet-le-Duc and Ruskin, but his is not a comparative treatment, and his point of view also differs from mine.

8 What he did include may be of interest: Norman Shaw's Grimsdyke of 1872, a house by Burges at Cardiff, one of Wilkinson's North Oxford houses and three cottages in Oxfordshire by him, Waterhouse's Master's Lodging at Pembroke College in Cambridge and Colonel Edis's Boscombe Spa Hotel of 1873 at Bournemouth. See *Habitations Modernes*, Paris 1875.

9 Paul Gout, *Viollet-le-Duc*, 1914, p. 64.

10 Sir Kenneth Clark, *op. cit.* p. xv.

11 Gout, *op. cit.* p. 133.

12 *Ibid.* p. 70.

13 Ruskin, *Lib. Ed.* VIII, 56.

14 *Ibid.* 60 and 78, etc.

15 *Ibid.* 83.

16 Viollet-le-Duc, *Entretiens*, Paris 1863, V, 451.

17 *Ibid.* II, 120.

18 *Ibid.* I, 472.

19 Viollet-le-Duc, *Revue Générale d' Architecture*, X, 379.

20 In this statement, incidentally, Viollet follows Victor Hugo who in his famous architectural chapter in *Notre Dame de Paris* (Book III, Chap. 1) speaks of the building as an 'œuvre colossale d'un homme et d'un peuple, tout ensemble une et complexe comme l'Iliade et les romanzeros'.

21 Ruskin, *The Stones of Venice, Lib. Ed.* X, 213.

22 Ruskin, *The Queen of the Air, Lib. Ed.* XIX, 389.

23 Ruskin, *Seven Lamps, Lib. Ed.* VIII, 218.

24 *Ibid.* 28–9.

25 *Ibid.* 11.

26 *Ibid.* 11.

27 Ruskin, *The Elements of Drawing,* 1857, *Lib. Ed.* XV, 82.

28 Ruskin, *The Stones of Venice, Lib. Ed.* X, 201.

29 *Ibid.* 184, etc., also 204.

30 *Ibid.* 202–3.

31 *Ibid.* 204.

32 *Ibid.* 215.

33 *Ibid.* 239.

34 *Ibid.* 239–40.

35 *Ibid.* 243–4.

36 *Ibid.* 268–9.

37 *Ibid.* 182.

38 Ruskin, *Seven Lamps, Lib. Ed.* VIII, 190.

39 *Ibid.* 225.

40 *Ibid.* 233–4.

41 *Ibid.* 252, 253, 255.

42 *Ibid.* 258.

43 *Ibid.* 251, 256.

44 Gout, *op. cit.* p. 92, and in many other places.

45 Viollet-le-Duc, *Dictionnaire.* Introduction, 1854, p. xviii.

46 Gout, *op. cit.* p. 92.

47 R. Middleton, 'The Abbé de Cordemoy and the Graeco-Gothic Ideal', in *The Journal of the Warburg and Courtauld Institutes*, XXV, 1962 and XXVI, 1963.

48 'L'art national et l'art étranger', and 'Du style gothique au XIXe siècle' in *Annales Archéologiques*, II, 1845 and IV, 1846.

49 Viollet-le-Duc, *Entretiens*, I, 32.

50 *Ibid.* 451, etc.

51 Viollet-le-Duc, *Habitations Modernes*, Paris 1875, p. 2.

52 Viollet-le-Duc, *Entretiens*, I, 478; *Les Eglises de Paris*, Paris 1883, though the notes were not written by Viollet who had, it will be remembered, died in 1879.

53 Viollet-le-Duc, *Entretiens*, I, 388.

54 *Ibid.* II, 67 and 55.

55 I must humbly confess that I have been unable to find from my extracts and notes where this passage occurs.

56 Ruskin, *Modern Painters*, V, 1860, *Lib. Ed.* VII, 425.

57 Ruskin, *Val d'Arno*, 1874, *Lib. Ed.* XXIII, 162.

58 Ruskin, *The Crown of Wild Olive*, *Lib. Ed.* XVIII, 414.

59 Ruskin, *Seven Lamps*, *Lib. Ed.* VIII, 159–60.

60 *Ibid.* 28.

61 *Ibid.* 68.

62 *Ibid.* 66.

63 *Ibid.* 67.

64 I have dealt with all this in my *Pioneers of Modern Design* (current Pelican edition 1960); so have others.

65 Viollet-le-Duc, *Entretiens*, II, etc., 125, etc., in fact the whole of *Entretiens*, XII.

66 *Ibid.* 310, etc. Viollet here already mentions (p. 334) Saulnier's factory for Chocolat Meunier at Noisiel, discussed and illustrated so prominently in Giedion's *Space, Time and Architecture*.

67 *Ibid.* 336.

68 Ruskin, *Lib. Ed.* IX, 456.

69 Ruskin, *Seven Lamps*, *Lib. Ed.* VIII, 242.

70 Viollet-le-Duc, *Dictionnaire*, VIII, 1866, p. 14.

71 Ruskin, *Seven Lamps*, *Lib. Ed.* VIII, 242.

72 For all these see my *Pioneers*; see Note 64.

73 Ruskin, *Lib. Ed.* XXXVII, 243.

LIST AND SOURCES OF ILLUSTRATIONS

1 John Everett Millais: John Ruskin, 1853–4. Oil on canvas. *Mrs Patrick Gibson*

2 Eugène Viollet-le-Duc. About 1840. Daguerrotype. *Courtesy Madame Geneviève Viollet le Duc*

3 Ruskin: study of a piece of rock with quartz veining. Watercolour. *The Ruskin Galleries, Bembridge School, Isle of Wight*

4 Ruskin: mountain rocks and Alpine rose. Watercolour. *The Ruskin Galleries, Bembridge School, Isle of Wight*

5 Ruskin: pine forest on Mont-Cenis. Lampblack. *Ashmolean Museum, Oxford*

6 Ruskin: Glacier des Bossons, Chamonix. 1854. Ink, pencil and wash. *Ashmolean Museum, Oxford*

7 The Ruskin Road at Hinksey. 1874. Photograph. *The Ruskin Galleries, Bembridge School, Isle of Wight*

8 Viollet-le-Duc: Innsbruck, with the Brenner Pass in the distance. 1854. Pencil. *Fonds Viollet-le-Duc. Archives Photographiques*

9 Viollet-le-Duc: Gothic cathedral. From *Dictionnaire raisonné de l'architecture française*, 1858–68

10 Ruskin: St Mary's tower and All Souls College, Oxford. 1880. Pencil. *Courtauld Institute Galleries (Witt Collection), London*

11 Ruskin: Church of Notre-Dame, Saint-Lô. 1848. Pencil and brown wash. *Fogg Art Museum, Harvard University (gift of Samuel Sachs)*

12 Viollet-le-Duc: Angel Choir, Lincoln Cathedral. 1850. Pencil. *Fonds Viollet-le-Duc. Archives Photographiques*

13 Ruskin: part of the façade of the Doge's Palace. 1845. Wash drawing. *Ashmolean Museum, Oxford*

14 Viollet-le-Duc: diagrammatic section through a Venetian palazzo (detail). From *Entretiens sur l'architecture*, 1863

15 Ruskin: Iris Florentina. 1871. Pencil and watercolour. *Ashmolean Museum, Oxford*

16 Ruskin: capital, Doge's Palace, Venice. Wash, pencil and ink. *The Ruskin Galleries, Bembridge School, Isle of Wight*

17 Ruskin: moss and wild strawberry. 1880. Pencil and body colour. *Ashmolean Museum, Oxford*

18 Ruskin: apse of the Cathedral at Pisa. 1872. Pencil and watercolour. *Ashmolean Museum, Oxford*

19 Ruskin: Santa Maria della Spina, Pisa. 1840. Pencil and watercolour. *Courtauld Institute Galleries (Witt Collection), London*

20 Ruskin: Casa Contarini-Fasan. 1841. Pencil and wash. *Ashmolean Museum, Oxford*

21 Viollet-le-Duc: west front of Saint-Denys-de-l'Estrée, Saint-Denis. 1864–67. *Arts Graphiques de la Cité*

22 Viollet-le-Duc: interior of Saint-Denys-de-l'Estrée, Saint-Denis. 1864–67. *Archives Photographiques, Paris*

23 Viollet-le-Duc: project for a market place. From *Entretiens sur l'architecture*, 1863

24 Viollet-le-Duc: project for a vaulted hall. From *Entretiens sur l'architecture*, 1863

25 Viollet-le-Duc: design for flats in the Rue de Douai, Paris, *c.* 1860. *Archives Photographiques*

26 Viollet-le-Duc: project for the Opéra, Paris. 1860. Watercolour. *Direction de l'Architecture. Archives Photographiques*

27 Viollet-le-Duc: design for the west front of the Cathedral of Clermont-Ferrand. 1864. Pen and watercolour. *Direction de l'Architecture. Archives Photographiques*

28 Château de Pierrefonds in 1855. *Direction de l'Architecture. Archives Photographiques*

29 Château de Pierrefonds as it is now. *Giraudon*

30, 31 Viollet-le-Duc: sketch of the walls of Carcassonne before restoration, and proposed restorations. About 1853. *Archives Photographiques*

32 Carcassonne from the air. *Greff*